I0813916

THE POCKET

Greek Mythology

Published in 2026
by Gemini Gift Books
Part of Gemini Books Group

Based in Woodbridge and London

Marine House, Tide Mill Way
Woodbridge, Suffolk IP12 1AP
United Kingdom

www.geminibooks.com

Part of the Gemini Pockets series

Text by Malcolm Croft

ISBN 978-1-80247-316-2

A CIP catalogue record for this book is available from the British Library.

Manufacturer's EU Representative: Eurolink Compliance Limited, 25 Herbert Place, Dublin, D02 AY86, Republic of Ireland. admin@eurolink-europe.ie.

Printed in China

10 9 8 7 6 5 4 3 2 1

Picture Credits: Alamy/BE&W agencja fotograficzna Sp. z o.o.: front cover, p3; Shutterstock: aln_dek 54; Arthur Balitskii 37; Chorna_black 32–3, 59, 86–7, 108–9, 124; darko m 18, 29, 42, 46, 48, 52, 56, 61, 84, 89, 90, 92, 101; delcarmat 4, 12, 23, 25, 71, 90, 95, 97, 99, 102, 126; Elena Sazanova 7, 11, 14, 20,26,30, 36, 45, 50, 55, 74, 77, 81, 82, 91, 115, 118, 121, 125, 128; Eroshka 41matrioshka 8; Hoika Mikhail 15, 22, 68, 120; Natalllenka.m 72, 73, 113; Nature line 40, 105; Svetolk 9, 10, 16, 17, 21, 35, 43, 57, 62, 64, 65, 76, 78, 85, 103, 106, 111, 116, 119.

THE POCKET

Greek Mythology

Contents

INTRODUCTION

Today, the world is experiencing a Greek mythology renaissance. They're everywhere. Again. From cinematic superheroes to modern adaptations, from William Shakespeare to Christopher Nolan, Greek legends continue to demand our attention, offering us a glimpse of our storytelling past and an instruction manual for our future. The world will eternally crave these timeless tales.

While today the word "myth" is pretty synonymous with "fiction", in antiquity – around 5,000 years ago – myths were, in fact, an alternate form of reality. They explained the things that the ancient Greeks could not understand – the origin of the cosmos and the earth, as well as natural forces, and so the existence of powers beyond human control. More than just stories, they were life and death personified, and still such myths endure as they continue to influence our wordsmiths and visionaries today.

This compact but comprehensive compendium presents the key legendary figures, terrifying creatures and immortal gods of these ancient times, when Zeus and his dysfunctional family ruled the earth, the heavens – and beyond. Let's celebrate their powerful legacy!

"No man or woman born, coward or brave, can shun his destiny."

The Iliad, Homer, 750 BCE

CHAPTER ONE

Chaos & Creation

Oral Tradition

Ancient Greek origin myths began over 5,000 years ago, not from a single creator but from a collection of oral stories compiled and refined by poets, playwrights and philosophers, such as Aeschylus, Sophocles, Euripides and Aristophanes. These myths likely evolved from tales originating in the Bronze Age Minoan civilization of Crete, Europe's first human civilization, which flourished from roughly 3000 to 1100 BCE.

In the Beginning

Greek mythology states that before the universe, only Chaos existed – a primordial void. From this nothingness arose the primordial forces of creation: Gaia (Earth), Uranus (Sky), Tartarus (Punishment), Eros (Desire), Nyx (Night), Hemera (Day) and Aether (Heaven). These first beings represented the fundamental cosmic building blocks for the ancient Greeks. Everything else, including gods, monsters and mortals, descended from them.

"Think not to match yourself against the gods, for men that walk the earth cannot hold their own with the immortals."

The Iliad, Homer, 750 BCE

Rise of the Titans

Born of Uranus (Sky) and Gaia (Earth), the 12 Titans were the first generation of gods that ruled the universe after the age of the primordial forces came to an end. The Titans represented a new "golden age", and while they too defined the essential elements of the cosmos, they also embodied the eternal cycle of creation and destruction, rebellion and succession – and outgrowing your parents. When the Titans were eventually defeated, they were sent to live in Hades' Underworld for eternity.

Meet the Titans...

1. CRONUS: Ruler of the universe and time
2. RHEA: Goddess of fertility
3. OCEANUS: God of the sea and water
4. TETHYS: Goddess of fresh water
5. HYPERION: God of light and observation
6. THEIA: Goddess of the sun and light
7. COEUS: God of the oracles, wisdom and foresight
8. PHOEBE: Goddess of prophecy and intellect
9. MNEMOSYNE: Goddess of memory
10. THEMIS: Goddess of law, order and justice
11. CRIUS: God of constellations
12. IAPETUS: God of mortal life or god of death

"No fable made famous by the Greeks is to be neglected."

Philosophumena, Hippolytus of Rome,
early 3rd century AD

The Titanomachy

The biggest of all of the mythological conflicts was the Titanomachy, the epic decade-long cosmic battle royale between the 12 Titans and their offspring – the 12 Olympians. The Titans were led by Cronus. The Olympians were commanded by Cronus's son, Zeus. The war erupted when Zeus and his Olympian siblings challenged the ruling Titans for universal supremacy. Fuelled by resentment against their father Cronus, who had swallowed his first five children (but not Zeus), the Olympians battled the Titans in a clash of primordial powers. Ultimately, the Olympians, with Zeus's thunderbolts, prevailed, imprisoning the defeated Titans in Tartarus. This victory established the Olympian gods as the new rulers of the cosmos, ushering in a new era of divine order.

The Gigantomachy

Enraged by the Olympian victory in the Titanomachy, the Gigantes – huge monstrous creatures born from the blood of Uranus, with long serpentine legs – decided to fight back. A colossal war ensued across the cosmos. With the help of the Olympian mortal hero Heracles, who possessed poison arrows, the Olympians defeated the Gigantes also, with many furious giants left either dead or imprisoned beneath volcanoes (hence eruptions). The Gigantomachy solidified the Olympians' dominance over the world – never to be challenged again (until Christianity, of course).

The Age of Olympians

The fruit of Cronus and Rhea's loins, the Olympians represent a younger generation of immortals whom, unlike the Titans, were more active in the ruling of earth below, often intervening in the lives of mortals.

Meet the Olympians…

1. ZEUS: King of the gods, thunder, lightning and law and order
2. HERA: Queen of the gods, marriage and childbirth
3. POSEIDON: God of the sea, earthquakes, storms and horses
4. HADES: God of the Underworld and wealth
5. DEMETER: Goddess of agriculture and harvest
6. ATHENA: Goddess of wisdom and warfare
7. APOLLO: God of light and the sun
8. ARTEMIS: Goddess of the moon and hunting
9. ARES: God of war and violence
10. APHRODITE: Goddess of love and beauty, pleasure and procreation
11. HEPHAESTUS: God of fire, metal and volcanoes
12. HERMES: Messenger of the gods, commerce and sports

"The son of Cronos spoke, and bowed his dark brow in assent, and the ambrosial locks waved from the king's immortal head; and he made great Olympus quake."

The Iliad, Homer, 750 BCE

Mount Olympus

Mount Olympus, Greece's highest point at 2,917 meters, rises between Thessaly and Macedonia. Its three prominent peaks – Mytikas, Skolio and Stefani ("Zeus's throne") – pierce the clouds. Greek legend places the 12 Olympian gods atop Olympus, a revered, cloud-shrouded heavenly realm inaccessible to mere mortals, symbolizing the divide between gods and humans. Mount Olympus is where the gods convened on cosmic and mortal affairs.

Statue of Zeus

Considered one of the Seven Wonders of the Ancient World, the Statue of Zeus, located in the Temple of Zeus at Olympia, was a monumental chryselephantine (gold and ivory) statue, created by Phidias around 435 BC. It depicted Zeus seated on a throne adorned with gold and precious stones. When the Roman general Aemilius Paullus saw it, he was moved to his soul, "As if I had seen the god in person". It was that good. Unfortunately, the statue was lost, possibly dismantled, sometime around the 6th century AD, never to be seen again – *yet*.

Athena

Athens, Greece's capital city (today visited by over six million tourists annually), takes its name from Athena, the goddess of wisdom. Myth recounts her victory over Poseidon, god of the sea, in a contest for the city's patronage. Poseidon offered a saltwater spring by striking the Acropolis with his trident, symbolizing strength. Athena presented an olive tree, representing peace and wisdom. The citizens, led by King Cecrops, deemed Athena's gift superior, naming the city Athens in her honour, and in doing so, emphasizing peace over brute force. An olive tree still stands proudly on the north side of the Acropolis today.

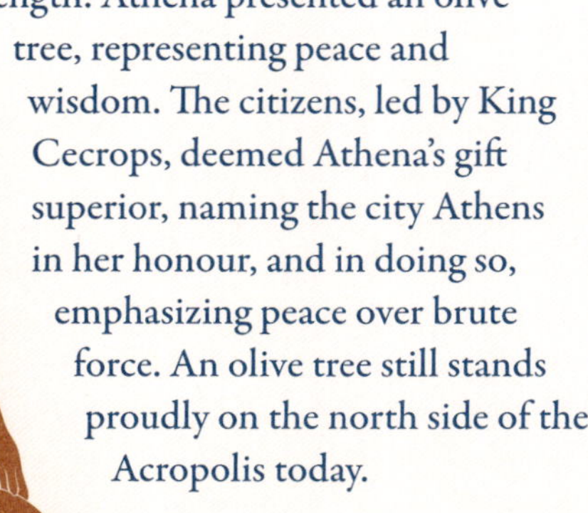

Prometheus

"I gave them fire… and with it, all the arts of civilization."

Prometheus in *Theogony*, Hesiod, 700 BCE

In Greek mythology, Prometheus, a powerful Titan (son of Iapetus), was known for his foresight and deep love of humanity. Defying the Olympian gods, he daringly stole fire from their divine forge and gifted it to humankind. This act enabled humans to generate warmth, smelt metals for tools, and ultimately develop the foundations of technology, knowledge and civilization. Enraged by this defiance, Zeus chained Prometheus in the Caucasus Mountains, where an eagle daily devoured his liver for 30 years. For his courageous act of theft on behalf of humanity, Prometheus became an enduring symbol of defiance against tyranny and a champion of human progress.

The Muses

The nine daughters of Zeus, king of the gods, and Mnemosyne, the goddess of memory, are revered collectively as the Nine Muses, goddesses of the arts, music and poetry, who were believed to inspire artistic creativity in mortals by whispering inspiration in their ears. In fact, the very word "museum" comes from the Greek "mouseion", meaning "place of the muses". Which muse inspired you?

1. CALLIOPE: Muse of poetry and eloquence
2. CLIO: Muse of history
3. ERATO: Muse of lyric and love poetry
4. EUTERPE: Muse of music
5. MELPOMENE: Muse of tragedy
6. POLYHYMNIA: Muse of hymns and mime
7. TERPSICHORE: Muse of dance and choral song
8. THALIA: Muse of comedy and idyllic poetry
9. URANIA: Muse of astronomy and astrology

The Fates

"Even the gods cannot escape what is spun."
The Odyssey, Homer, 750 BCE

Meet Clotho, Lachesis and Atropos – the Moirai – the three powerful goddesses of fate and destiny in Greek mythology. Not even the gods could alter their judgment, as these sisters, often depicted weaving, ensured mortals lived their predetermined lives. Clotho, "the spinner", created life by spinning its thread. Lachesis, "the allotter", measured the thread's length, determining lifespan. And Atropos, "the inflexible", cut the thread, signifying death and its manner. The myth is responsible for the idiom "Hanging by a thread", to signify a precarious situation where a negative outcome seems imminent.

"The woman took off the great lid of the jar with her hands and scattered all these and her thought caused sorrow and mischief to men."

Works and Days, Hesiod, 700 BCE

Pandora's Box

"Zeus, who guided mortals to be wise, has established his fixed law – wisdom comes through suffering."

Oresteia, Aeschylus, 458 BCE

Seeking revenge for Prometheus's fire theft – a gift for humanity – an enraged Zeus orchestrated the creation of Pandora, the first human woman out of soil and water by Hephaestus, the god of fire and sculpture. Each Olympian bestowed upon Pandora a gift, hence her name, meaning "all-gifts" in Greek. (Athena gave Pandora wisdom, Aphrodite beauty, Hermes cunning, and so on.) Zeus presented Pandora with a sealed jar, strictly forbidding her from opening it. However, Pandora's irresistible human curiosity eventually overcame her. She opened the jar… and all manner of evils – sorrow, disease, envy, pain – escaped, plaguing humanity for eternity. Only hope remained trapped inside, offering a bittersweet solace in the face of worldly suffering. Pandora's Box serves as a reminder for the presence of evil in the world, while also lumbering one woman with the unfair burden of blame… even though it was all Zeus's fault.

Delphi

At the sacred Temple of Apollo at Delphi, on Mount Parnassus in Central Greece, you'll find 147 Delphic Maxims, a set of moral teachings that the priestess Pythia, the Oracle of Apollo, believed to be the most valuable lessons from Greek culture. Some of the best-known maxims, quoted below, are believed to have been authored by Apollo, the god of light himself, and are prominently located at the entrance to the temple.

"Know thyself"

"Know your limits"

"Commit yourself emphatically"

"Follow the gods"

"Obey the law"

"Respect your parents"

"If you are a stranger, act like one"

"Long for wisdom"

“We are three brothers born by Rhea to Cronos, Zeus, and I, and the third is Hades, lord of the dead men. All was divided among us three ways, each given his domain. Hades drew the lot of the mists and the darkness, and Zeus was allotted the wide sky.”

Poseidon in *The Iliad*, Homer, 750 BCE

Hades

The original devil, the god of the Underworld and ruler of the realm of the dead, Hades, along with Zeus and Poseidon, is known as one of the "big three" brothers of Greek mythology. Unfortunately, it was he who drew the short straw and was granted dominion of the first incarnation of hell. Thankfully, he had a pet to keep himself company in the dark – a three-headed dog known as Cerberus – as well as Persephone, his wife, whom he abducted from the world above to be his queen.

According to ancient Greek legend, the entrance to the Underworld – the dominion of Hades – can be found underneath the 32-mile-long Acheron River in the Epirus region of northwest Greece, infamously known as the infernal River of Woe. It is here that a Charon, or ferryman, known as a psychopomp, carries the souls of the deceased into the afterlife. Also located within the Underworld was the realm where the souls of the most virtuous and heroic individuals resided. This paradise of eternal happiness and peace was known as Elysian Fields, or Elysium. Today, the Acheron River is popular for birdwatching, river trekking and zip lining.

The A to Z of Mythology: Part I

Many of our everyday English words and phrases are derived from Greek mythology...

- **Achilles' heel:** Weak spot (from Achilles, a Greek hero of the Trojan War, invincible except for his heel).
- **Aphrodisiac:** Arousing desire (from Aphrodite, the goddess of love, beauty, pleasure and procreation).
- **Apollonian:** Orderly, rational (from Apollo, the god of music, arts, knowledge, healing and prophecy, associated with order and reason).
- **Arachne:** Spider-related (from Arachne, a skilled weaver who challenged Athena; she was transformed into a spider as punishment).
- **Atlas:** Map collection (from Atlas, a Titan condemned by Zeus to hold up the celestial heavens on his shoulders).
- **Atrophy:** Wasting away (from Atropos, one of the three Fates who was tasked with choosing the manner of a person's death).

⁂ **Cereal:** Grain food (from Ceres, the Roman name for Demeter, the goddess of agriculture, harvest and nurture).

⁂ **Chronology:** Time order (from Chronos, the primordial god of time).

⁂ **Cloth:** Thread of life (from Clotho, one of the three Fates, who spun the thread of a person's life).

⁂ **Dionysian:** Chaotic, emotional (from Dionysus, god of wine, revelry and theatre; associated with irrationality and passion).

⁂ **Echo:** Repeated sound (from Echo, a nymph cursed by Hera to only be able to repeat the last words of others).

⁂ **Fury:** Rage (from the Furies, chthonic goddesses of vengeance, particularly for crimes against natural order and family).

⁂ **Herculean:** Very strong (from Heracles, later romanized as Hercules, a hero renowned for his strength and feats).

Hesiod

Hesiod's 8th-century BCE poem, *Theogony* (or "birth of the gods"), is a foundational Greek mythological text. Alongside Homer's *The Iliad*, it first narrated the cosmos's and primordial gods' origins, outlining a divine family tree leading to Zeus's reign. *Theogony* shaped ancient Greek understanding of the universe, the gods, and their relationships, influencing poetry, philosophy, science and agriculture. Notably, it was the first text to describe the universe emerging from nothing, a concept later supported by the 1931 Big Bang Theory.

Written around 700 BCE, Hesiod's *Works and Days* outlined the "Five Ages of Man": Golden, Silver, Bronze, Heroic and Iron. The Golden Age, under Cronus's rule, was a time of peace, abundance and immortality. The Silver Age, ruled by Zeus, introduced seasons and agriculture, but also impiety. The Bronze Age featured violent, warlike figures. The Heroic Age included brave protagonists from the Trojan War. The current Iron Age is characterized by toil, suffering and moral decay, a state Hesiod lamented and predicted would unravel humanity.

Homer

Little is known of Homer, the great Greek poet, yet his work preserved Greek mythology so it could echo for eternity. Believed to have lived and worked in Ithaca (possibly in modern-day Turkey), he's credited with the 8th century BCE epics *The Iliad* – one of the oldest surviving texts in Europe – which recounts the Trojan War's final year and Achilles' wrath against King Agamemnon; as well as *The Odyssey*, which details Odysseus's ten-year journey home to Ithaca after the war.

For over 2,000 years, Greek myths were orally transmitted. It wasn't until Greece's Archaic Period (*c.* 800–480 BCE) and the creation of the Greek alphabet in 1000 BCE that authors such as Homer and Hesiod began writing the stories down. Adapted from Phoenician script, the Greek alphabet's crucial innovation was the addition of vowels, making it the first true alphabet. In fact, the word "alphabet" itself originates from its first two letters: alpha and beta.

"Trojans, don't trust this horse. What ever it is, I'm afraid of Greeks, even those bearing gifts."

The Aeneid, Book II, Virgil, *c.* 19 BCE

The Trojan Horse

Perhaps the most famous Greek myth of all… As recounted in Homer's *The Iliad*, Sparta's King Menelaus sent his entire war fleet across the Aegean Sea to retrieve his queen, Helen. After a decade-long stalemate in the Trojan War, the Greeks deceptively left a massive wooden horse as a supposed peace offering at the city gates. Inside, elite warriors like Odysseus, who was the mastermind behind the plan, Diomedes, Neoptolemus, Menelaus and Ajax lay hidden. The curious Trojans brought the horse into their city. At night, the Greeks emerged, opened the gates for the returning army, and Troy was destroyed!

Sparta

"What happened in my heart,
to make me leave my home.
And my own land, to follow where a stranger led?
Rail at the goddess; be more resolute than Zeus,
Who holds power over all other divinities
But is himself the slave of love. Show Aphrodite
Your indignation; me, pardon and sympathy."

Helen of Troy in *Troades*, Euripides, 415 BCE

Sparta, in the Peloponnese region of southern Greece, was home to Princess Helen, daughter of Zeus and Queen Leda, and infamously known as "Helen of Troy", despite being from Sparta. Alongside Athens, Corinth and Thebes, Sparta was a major ancient Greek city-state. The word "laconic" derives from Sparta's location in Laconia, as its people were known for their brief, direct speech. A famous example: when Philip II of Macedon threatened, "If I invade Laconia, I shall turn you out", the Spartans simply replied, "If." Iconic indeed.

Ithaca

"I am Odysseus, known to the world for every kind of craft – my fame has reached the skies. Sunny Ithaca is my home."

Odysseus in *The Odyssey*, Homer, 750 BCE

Welcome to Ithaca – the sun-soaked, legendary home of Odysseus from Homer's *The Odyssey*. After the Trojan War and a decade-long journey, Odysseus's return symbolizes his reward for his determination and dedication. While the epic's Ithaca is likely fictional, a real Ionian island off Kefalonia shares the name and has long been associated with the mythological Greek location. You too can journey there. Why not visit Vathy Harbour, Filiatro Beach, Polis Bay, the Cave of the Nymphs, "Homer's old school", and the Acropolis of Aetos. All are famous landmarks.

Fountains and Springs

In Greek mythology, magic fountains appear several times as sources of wonder. The Fountain of Youth, a popular narrative in literature, first appeared in Greek mythology in the writings of Greek historian Herodotus in 500 BCE, who teased the world of a spring that gave visitors eternal life. However, it is the Fountain of Salmacis that is perhaps the most famed in Greek legend.

Hermaphroditus, son of Hermes and Aphrodite, inherited his parents' beauty. At 15, he journeyed to Halicarnassus (modern-day Turkey). As he drank from a spring, a water nymph, Salmacis, was instantly smitten with him. He rejected her advances but, later, as he bathed in the spring, Salmacis jumped in and begged the gods for them to be bound together forever. They granted her wish and their bodies fused into one being of both sexes.

Europa

Europe, the continent, takes its name from the famous Greek myth of Europa, a Phoenician princess revered for her radiant beauty. Her looks captivated Zeus, the king of the gods. To woo her, he transformed himself into a magnificent, gentle white bull. Entranced by the bull's docile nature, she climbed onto its back. Suddenly, the bull charged into the ocean, carrying the terrified Europa across the Mediterranean Sea to Crete. There, Zeus revealed his true form and seduced her. Their love bore Zeus several famous sons, including King Minos. Europa became the first queen of Crete.

CHAPTER TWO

Gods & Heroes

King of the Gods

Zeus is the famous Olympian king of the gods, who ruled by wielding his primary weapon – a thunderbolt. It was Zeus that masterminded the Titanomachy, the ten-year war against the Titans to overthrow his parents, Cronus and Rhea. Across world mythologies, Zeus is just one of many immortals deemed god of gods. Here are a few equivalents:

⁂ **Jupiter**: Roman mythology

⁂ **Odin**: Norse mythology

⁂ **Amun**: Egyptian mythology

⁂ **Indra**: Hinduisim

⁂ **Perun**: Slavic mythology

⁂ **Dagda**: Celtic mythology

⁂ **Jade Emperor**: Chinese mythology

⁂ **Amaterasu-ōmikami**: Japanese mythology

⁂ **Ometeotl**: Aztec mythology

⁂ **Viracocha**: Inca mythology

"According to Greek mythology, humans were originally created with four arms, four legs and a head with two faces. Fearing their power, Zeus split them into two separate parts, condemning them to spend their lives in search of their other halves."

The Symposium, Plato, *c.* 370 BCE

Poseidon

Poseidon, the powerful and often volatile god of the sea, earthquakes and horses, ruled the oceans with his trident, commanding storms and calm. Known as the "earth-shaker", one of his prominent myths involves his pursuit of the Nereid Amphitrite. Wary of his temper, she fled to the sea's depths. Undeterred, Poseidon dispatched sea creatures to find her. A persuasive dolphin succeeded, and Amphitrite returned to become his queen, and the goddess of the sea. In gratitude, Poseidon immortalized the dolphin as the constellation Delphinus.

Atlas

"Atlas the baleful, he knows the depths of all the seas, and he, no other, holds up the tall pillars that keep the sky and earth apart."

The Odyssey, Homer, 750 BCE

A Titan god, Atlas was known for his immense strength and endurance during the Titanomachy. After the Olympians' victory over the Titans, Zeus punished Atlas for his role in the war by making him bear the weight of the heavens on his shoulders for eternity.

In 1569, Flemish cartographer Gerardus Mercator honoured Atlas by featuring him holding the world on his map collection's title page, naming the collection *Atlas*. This prominent depiction led to "atlas" becoming the standard term for a bound book of maps, fittingly linking the Titan's burden to the weight of the world's geographical knowledge contained within. Today, Mercator's Projection – a cylindrical map projection of the world – is still the standard map model used around the world.

Mighty Aphrodite

Aphrodite, the Olympian goddess of love and beauty (and fertility), emerged from the sea foam – *aphros*, in Greek – fully formed and breathtakingly beautiful. The wind then carried her to the shores of Cyprus, where upon reaching land, flowers sprang up beneath her feet, at once connecting the beauty of the land with the wonder of the sea.

The myth of Adonis and Aphrodite, the original "doomed lovers" narrative seen in twisted fairytales such as Romeo and Juliet, tells of the undying love between the handsome mortal Adonis and the immortal Olympian goddess of love, Aphrodite. Born from a myrrh tree, Adonis's beauty captivated her. After a series of interventions in their affair, culminating in the murder of Adonis by the jealous Ares, Adonis was forced to remain in the Underworld only for half of the year. But when Adonis and Aphrodite were together, the sun shone brightly and the soil was kind to the people, flowers bloomed and fruits ripened – such is the power of love.

"Even gods cannot escape love."

Homeric Hymn to Aphrodite, Homer, 700 BCE

Eros and Psyche

One day, a mortal called Psyche became revered as the most beautiful woman in the world. A jealous Aphrodite ordered her son Eros to make Psyche fall for a monster. But, distracted by Psyche's beauty, Eros pricked himself on his own arrow, and fell in love with Psyche instead. Keen for Psyche to never know his true immortal identity, or they would no longer be able to be together, Eros showered Psyche with riches in a hidden palace, visiting only at night and forbidding her to look at him. However, she did soon discover his identity. Desperate to be together still, Psyche visited the vengeful Aphrodite, who tasked her with a challenge: go to the Underworld and retrieve Persephone's box. Psyche was advised not to open it. However, she could not resist. Inside the box was Morpheus, the god of dreams, who plunged Psyche into a deep sleep. When Eros learned about his mother's tricks and Psyche's fate, he flew directly to Olympus and begged Zeus to save her. Zeus, touched by their love, not only woke Psyche up but also made her immortal, so she and Eros could be together forever.

Ares

"Ares (the God of War) hates those who hesitate."

Heracleidae, Euripides, 430 BCE

Ares, the Greek god of war, was one of the 12 Olympian gods, and represented the brutal and violent aspects of warfare. While his sister Athena embodied the more strategic aspects of war and wisdom, Ares was seen as a more reckless source of power, as shown in *The Iliad*.

Helios

"Helios the Sun rides his chariot... he rests there upon the highest point of heaven, until he marvellously drives them down again through heaven to Oceanus."

Homeric Hymn to Helios, Homer, 700 BCE

Unable to explain its existence, the ancient Greeks believed that the Sun was a chariot driven across the sky by the god Helios. Phaethon, Helios's son, drunk on youthful arrogance, secretly took the chariot for a spin one day; lacking his father's strength and skill, Phaethon quickly lost control of the powerful, fiery steeds and knocked the Sun chariot out of the sky, ultimately scorching the earth below. Deserts were the everlasting result. Angry, Zeus came down from Mount Olympus and struck down Phaethon with a thunderbolt.

Demeter

Persephone, daughter of the goddess Demeter and Zeus, was abducted by Hades, the god of the Underworld, who was smitten by her beauty. As recounted in the *Homeric Hymn to Demeter*, Persephone was gathering flowers with ocean nymphs when, drawn to a wondrous narcissus flower, the earth split open. Hades emerged in his golden chariot and stole Persephone away to the Underworld.

Demeter searched tirelessly for her lost daughter, causing the earth's fertility to wane. Witnessing Demeter's sorrow, the Sun revealed Hades' deed. The goddess then confronted Zeus, demanding that Persephone be returned or else she would not let the earth blossom again. The princess was returned. Persephone's time in the Underworld each year corresponds to the barrenness of winter, while her return to her mother, brings the growth and life of spring and summer, explaining the seasons to the ancient Greeks.

"Queen Demeter, bringer of seasons and giver of good gifts, what god of heaven or what mortal man has rapt away Persephone and pierced with sorrow your dear heart?"

Homeric Hymn to Demeter, Homer, 700 BCE

Dionysus

Dionysus, the Olympian god of wine (and, fittingly, madness and wild frenzy) was the son of Zeus and the mortal princess, Semele. Dionysus' birth was dramatic: Semele perished after seeing Zeus in his divine form, but the unborn Dionysus was saved when Zeus gestated him in his thigh, earning him the title "twice-born", the meaning of Dionysus. The god of wine travelled the world extensively, spreading the cultivation of the vine, as well as the joy and liberation that comes with wine-induced ecstasy. Three cheers for Dionysus!

The Midas Touch

King Midas, a wealthy ruler of Phrygia, once treated Silenus, the companion of Dionysus, the god of wine, with kindness. As gratitude for his benevolence, Dionysus offered Midas any wish. Midas wished that everything he touched would turn to gold, and it did! But his joy soon turned to despair; food and drink became inedible gold, so too did the outside world. Realizing his foolishness, Midas pleaded with Dionysus to reverse his wish. Taking pity, the god instructed Midas to bathe in the River Pactolus. As Midas swam, the golden touch flowed out into the river, turning its banks golden and freeing Midas from his curse. The moral of this myth? Be careful what you wish for.

Hera

"Heaven has no rage like love to hatred turned, nor hell a fury like a woman scorned."

The Mourning Bride, William Congreve, 1697

Hera, queen of the gods and goddess of marriage, was perpetually incensed by the infidelities of Zeus, her husband and brother. One tale of her wicked wrath involves Io, a beautiful priestess. To hide their affair, Zeus shrouded Io in a cloud, but Hera's suspicion led Zeus to transform Io into a white heifer. No fool, Hera demanded the cow as a gift. Zeus complied, and Hera assigned the hundred-eyed monster, the Argus Panoptes, to guard her, preventing any reunion. Heartbroken, Zeus sent Hermes to kill Argus, freeing Io. Enraged by Argus's death, Hera tormented Io with a gadfly, driving her far away across the globe until she found solace in Egypt. This is just one of many of Hera's relentless acts of vengeance against Zeus's lovers, a constant theme in Greek mythology.

Apollo and Daphne

Spare a thought for Apollo and Daphne; their myth is indeed hard to swallow. Daphne, a beautiful water nymph and daughter of a river god, one day caught the eye of Apollo, the god of light. However, the fiercely independent Daphne had vowed to a life of celibacy. The mischievous Eros, god of desire, intervened. He shot Apollo with a golden arrow, igniting an unquenchable passion, while simultaneously striking Daphne with a leaden arrow, filling her with a complete loathing for the relentless Apollo. The pair were bound together in an eternal cycle of unwanted desire: Apollo forever spurned and Daphne forever chased. Thankfully, Daphne is eventually freed from Eros's curse and is transformed into a Laurel tree (with which Apollo remains obsessed).

Actaeon and Artemis

"I am Actaeon! Know your own master!"

Metamorphoses, Ovid, 8 BCE

As masterfully recounted in Ovid's *Metamorphoses*, the tale of Actaeon and Artemis serves as a stark (naked) reminder of the chasm separating mortals and immortals in Greek mythology. A skilled archer, Actaeon was hunting with his hounds one day when he inadvertently came upon Artemis, the goddess of the moon and the hunt, bathing nude in a secluded grove. Entranced by Artemis's beautiful naked form, Actaeon could not avert his gaze. Enraged by this violation of her privacy, Artemis instantly transformed him into a deer. No longer human and unable to communicate, Actaeon was then relentlessly pursued by his own pack of hunting dogs, who no longer recognized their master. They tore him apart.

Morpheus

Morpheus, in Greek mythology, is the god of dreams, specifically dreams that appear as human figures. As the son of Hypnos (the god of sleep) and Pasithea (the goddess of rest), Morpheus, whose name means "shape" or "form", can shape-shift and appear in dreams in the form of humans. The leader of the Oneiroi, the dream spirits, Morpheus has the ability to influence the dreams of gods too – much like he did in the myth of Alcyone and Ceyx.

Asclepius

"Gentle Asclepius, that craftsman of new health for weary limbs and banisher of pain, the godlike healer of all mortal sickness."

Pythian Ode, Pindar, 500 BCE

Asclepius, son of Apollo, the god of light, and the mortal Coronis, was the revered Greek god of medicine and healing. His extraordinary skill allowed him to even bring the dead back to life. This power, while aiding mortals, annoyed the hell out of Hades, the god of the Underworld, who regarded it as cheating! Concerned by this disruption and Hades' constant complaints, Zeus struck Asclepius down with a single thunderbolt. In retaliation for his son's death, an enraged Apollo murdered the Cyclopes, the race of one-eyed beings responsible for forging Zeus's all-powerful weapon of choice.

Narcissus and Echo

The love story of Narcissus and Echo is no Romeo and Juliet, but is an important Greek myth that serves as a cautionary tale about vanity and the pain of unrequited love. The talkative nymph Echo, cursed by Hera (for her incessant talking) to only repeat the words of others, loved the vain and self-obsessed human, Narcissus. Unable to express herself, Echo was cruelly rejected by Narcissus and faded away, leaving only her echo on the air. Punished for his self-love, Narcissus became fixated on his own reflection in a pool, and ultimately died from starvation. This myth gave power to the words "echo" and "narcissist".

Alcyone and Ceyx

The phrase "halcyon days", signifying a peaceful, happy period often tinged with nostalgia, comes from the Greek myth of Alcyone and Ceyx. Alcyone, daughter of Aeolus, god of the winds, married King Ceyx. After Ceyx's shipwreck death, a grieving Alcyone and Ceyx were transformed by Aeolus into halcyons (kingfishers) so they'd never be apart again. The myth states Aeolus calmed the winds and sea for 14 days around the winter solstice, allowing his daughter to safely lay her eggs on the water. (It should be noted, however, that kingfishers don't lay their eggs on water. They typically dig burrows in vertical banks of earth near rivers, streams, or other bodies of water...)

Heracles

You may know him better as Hercules – his Roman incarnation – but to the Greeks, Heracles was the strongest man to ever walk this earth. A demigod, Heracles was the offspring of a brief fling between Zeus and Alcmene, a mortal princess. Hated by Hera, the wife of Zeus, Hera sent two serpents to kill Heracles as a baby – but he strangled them! To get her revenge, she later drove Heracles mad, an act that led him to murder his wife and sons. To atone, he travelled to Delphi, Greece, and asked Apollo, god of knowledge, what he could do. Pythia, Apollo's oracle, told Heracles to serve his cousin, King Eurystheus, for 12 years. Eurystheus loathed Heracles too, so set 12 impossible tasks to complete all around the world, hoping he would perish. They were known as the 12 Labours of Heracles.

Using his superhuman strength, strategy, stealth and sheer stubbornness, Heracles completed all 12 labours, eventually freeing himself from the service of King Eurystheus and atoning for his family's death. After his death, Heracles was granted immortality and ascended to Mount Olympus, a testament to his heroic deeds.

The 12 Labours of Heracles were to...

1. Slay the Nemean Lion
2. Slay the nine-headed Lernaean hydra
3. Capture the golden hind of Artemis
4. Capture the Erymanthian boar
5. Clean the Augean stables in a single day
6. Slay the Stymphalian Birds
7. Capture the Cretan bull
8. Steal the mares of Diomedes
9. Obtain the Girdle of Hippolyta, Queen of the Amazons
10. Obtain the cattle of the monster Geryon
11. Steal the golden apples of the Hesperides
12. Capture and bring back Cerberus, the three-headed dog of Hades

Odysseus

Homer's epic poem, *The Odyssey*, written sometime around 800 BCE, is without a doubt the greatest story ever told, and certainly the origin of the Hero's Quest narrative. Consisting of more than 12,109 lines – or around 130,000 words – it was written in a meter of poetry known as dactylic hexameter, which lends a grand, stately rhythm to the narrative.

The plot: after the decade-long Trojan War, Odysseus is faced with another 10-year journey back home to Ithaca to see his beloved wife, Penelope. The voyage is filled with peril and challenges, all of which the hero must conquer. Along the way, Odysseus fights monsters (Cicones, the Lotus-Eaters, Polyphemus the Cyclops, Sirens, Scylla and Charybdis), supernatural beings (Circe, Calypso, Ghosts), gods (Poseidon's wrath) and temptations of immortality, other men (the 100 suitors vying for Penelope) and, finally, his own wife, who tests his true identity with cunning riddles and challenges.

Jason and the Golden Fleece

"I set out to commemorate the heroes of old who sailed the good ship Argo in quest of the Golden Fleece."

Jason in *Argonautica*, Apollonius Rhodius, 200 BCE

One of Greek mythology's most iconic tales is Jason's quest for the Golden Fleece, the fleece of a magical golden ram belonging to King Aeëtes, who kept it within a sacred grove, guarded by a sleepless dragon. For Jason, retrieving the fleece held immense significance, symbolizing ultimate wealth, power and his worthiness to claim the throne of Iolcus. His epic journey was fraught with peril, including encounters with murderous Lemnian women, foul harpies, the crushing Symplegades rocks, formidable Amazons, fire-breathing Colchian bulls, the monstrous Scylla and Charybdis, alluring sirens, the giant bronze automaton Talos and the dragon itself, not forgetting the powerful and ultimately vengeful sorceress Medea (who betrayed, killed Jason's children, murdered his wife, and then fled on a chariot pulled by dragons).

Theseus

Before sailing to Crete to face the Minotaur, Theseus agreed with his father, King Aegeus of Athens, to replace his ship's black sails with white upon his safe return. Aegeus anxiously watched for his son's ship. Despite slaying the Minotaur – with Ariadne's aid – and escaping the labyrinth, Theseus, in his excitement to return home, forgot to change the sails to white. Seeing the black sails across the sea, a heartbroken Aegeus atop the coast's edge presumed his son dead and threw himself into the rocks below. In his memory, that sea is now called the Aegean. Theseus became the new King of Athens.

Hector

"Life and death are balanced as it were on the edge of a razor."

The Iliad, Homer, 750 BCE

One of the most famous duels in Greek mythology pitted Troy's courageous hero, Hector, against the Greek hero Achilles. Driven by profound grief over Hector's killing of his beloved companion Patroclus, Achilles challenged Hector to single combat outside the gates of Troy. In this epic clash of two great warriors, Achilles relentlessly attacked Hector, striking the fatal blow and piercing his throat. Achilles' final words to Hector have echoed for eternity: "There can be no understanding between you and me, nor may there be any covenants between us, till one or other shall fall." *The Iliad* concludes with the solemn funeral rites for Hector.

Achilles

"Great Prince Achilles, your glory will live in our memory forever; your name will never die."

Agamemnon in *The Odyssey*, Homer, 750 BCE

Achilles, the celebrated Greek warrior of the Trojan War, was a demigod, son of the sea nymph Thetis and the mortal King Peleus. To confirm his immortality, Thetis dipped infant Achilles in the River Styx, one of the five rivers leading to the Underworld, holding him by his heel. This heel remained vulnerable, becoming his fatal weakness. After his triumph over Hector during their legendary duel, Achilles was felled by his brother Paris, whose arrow, guided by Zeus himself, pierced his unprotected heel. The "Achilles tendon" is the medical term for the tendon connecting the heel to the calf, an enduring reminder that Achilles' name will never die.

"Was this the face that launched a thousand ships And burnt the topless towers of Ilium?"

Faustus in *Doctor Faustus*,
Christopher Marlowe, 1588

Helen

Queen Helen of Sparta, famed as the most beautiful woman on earth, was married to Spartan King Menelaus. Her elopement with handsome Paris, Prince of Troy, Greek's bitter rivals, ignited the decade-long Trojan War. Led by King Agamemnon, the Greek forces, featuring heroes Achilles and Odysseus, battled King Priam and fierce Trojan warriors such as Hector. The epic siege drew the Olympian gods to intervene: Hera, Athena, Poseidon, Hephaestus and Hermes favoured the Greeks, while Aphrodite, Apollo, Ares and Artemis supported Troy. Zeus ultimately allowed Troy to fall.

The world-famous quote from Marlowe (see opposite), one of Elizabethan England's best-loved playwrights, second only to William Shakespeare, refers to Helen; Ilium was another name for the city of Troy.

Penelope

The myth of Odysseus and Penelope centres on enduring love and unwavering fidelity. While Odysseus battled in the Trojan War and faced a decade of perilous trials on his journey home, his wife Penelope faced her own challenges in Ithaca. Besieged by over a hundred insistent suitors vying for her hand and Odysseus's kingdom, she remained steadfastly loyal to her absent husband.

Penelope cleverly delayed her remarriage by claiming she would choose a suitor once she finished weaving a burial shroud for Odysseus's father, Laertes. Secretly, she unravelled her progress each night, a testament to her cunning and devotion. Despite years of uncertainty and pressure, Penelope never gave up hope for Odysseus's return. Their eventual reunion, after 20 long years, symbolizes the triumph of love and loyalty over adversity, solidifying Penelope as an icon of marital faithfulness.

"How I long for my husband – alive in memory, always, that great man."

Penelope in *The Odyssey*, Homer, 750 BCE

Cassandra

"Am I prophet of lies,
or a babbler from door to door?"

Cassandra in *Agamemnon*, Aeschylus, 1194

Cassandra, daughter of King Priam and Queen Hecuba of Troy, received the gift of prophecy from the god Apollo, who desired her love. When Cassandra rejected him, Apollo, unable to retract his divine gift, cursed her instead: her prophecies would always be true, but never believed. Cassandra foresaw Paris's abduction of Helen, the ruin of Troy, the treachery of the Trojan Horse and the tragic fate of Hector. Despite her desperate pleas and predictions, the Trojans dismissed her as mad, leading directly to the city's fall. And her own fatal fate. The Prophecy of Cassandra remains a potent symbol of the perils of ignored truth.

Amazonian Women

"When the Amazon women came, men's equals."
The Iliad, Homer, 750 BCE

A legendary race of fierce female warriors that lived in an independent kingdom on the fringes of the Greek world that excluded men – except for reproductive purposes – the Amazons were skilled in archery, horsemanship and combat. Their culture was a stark contrast to the patriarchal norms of ancient Greece, a rebellion against the male-dominated society and the atrocities of men, making their myths truly unique among the thousands of legends. Otrera, the first Amazon queen, was the offspring of Ares the god of war and the nymph Harmonia, making all Amazons demigoddesses.

In William Shakespeare's *Henry VI*, Charles VI of France famously referenced the Amazons, after losing a fight to Joan of Arc: "Stay, stay thy hands! Thou art an Amazon!" More recent references include the comic-book superhero Diana Prince – AKA Wonder Woman – who is the granddaughter of Otrera, and daughter of Hippolyta.

Oedipus

Born to Theban King Laius and Queen Jocasta, Oedipus's fate was doomed by a prophecy: he would kill his father and marry his mother. Abandoned as an infant to prevent this, he was rescued and raised by Corinthian royalty, Polybus and Merope. After learning of the prophecy, he fled Corinth to avoid the fate he believed applied to his adoptive parents. Along the way, Oedipus unknowingly killed Laius, his biological father, in a road dispute. Arriving in Thebes, plagued by the Sphinx, Oedipus solved her riddle, freed the city and became a hero. His reward? Marrying the widowed Queen Jocasta – his own mother. When she learnt the truth, she hanged herself, and fulfilled Oedipus's prophecy. The theory of the Oedipus complex, established by psychotherapist Sigmund Freud in the early 20th-century, is based on this scenario.

“People of Thebes, my countrymen, look on Oedipus. He solved the famous riddle, with his brilliance, he rose to power, a man beyond all power.”

Oedipus Rex, Sophocles, 429 BCE

“Daedalus saw the wings of his dear Icarus, floating on the waves; and he began to rail and curse his art.”

Metamorphoses, Ovid, 8 BCE

Daedalus

The famed labyrinth in Cretan King Minos's palace was designed by the Athenian inventor Daedalus. Minos commissioned Daedalus, and his son Icarus, to construct a labyrinth so complex it would trap a monster, called the Minotaur, forever. After completing the maze, King Minos imprisoned the pair inside the labyrinth in order to prevent knowledge of its exit from spreading. However, thanks to their brilliant minds, Daedalus and Icarus soon knew how to escape. They gathered fallen feathers from birds and glued them together with wax to make four large wings, two each. They tied the wings to each shoulder and then flew away from the maze. While in flight, Daedalus warned Icarus not to fly close to the sun because the wax would melt. Icarus, however, did not heed the warning. The hot sun softened the wax that held the feathers together and Icarus fell to the sea and drowned. Icaria, the Greek island in the Aegean Sea, is named after the spot where Icarus fell.

CHAPTER THREE

Monsters & Mythological Creatures

A to Z of Beasts

Greek mythology is filled with a feast of monstrous creatures let loose on a myriad mortal heroes, such as Odysseus, Perseus and Heracles. From dragons and serpents to giants and sirens, here are some favourites:

- **Automatons**: Metal creatures given life by Hephaestus.
- **Cerberus**: Three-headed hound guarding Hades' gates.
- **Charybdis**: A whirlpool-swirling sea monster.
- **Chimera**: Three-headed monster; lion foreparts, goat hindquarters and serpent-headed tail.
- **Cyclopes (Younger)**: Cannibalistic giants from Sicily.
- **Dracaena**: Female monsters with human heads/torsos and serpent tails.
- **Gigantes**: A hundred giants who warred against the gods.
- **Griffins**: Winged beasts with lion bodies.
- **Harpies**: Winged monsters with bird bodies and human female heads/torsos.

- **Hydra**: Nine-headed serpent; two grew back per decapitation.
- **Manticore**: Winged Persian monster with a human male head, a lion body and a spiked tail.
- **Minotaur**: Cretan monster with a bull's head and a human male body.
- **Monocerata**: Mythical horses with a single horn (known in Roman mythology as unicorni, hence the word unicorn).
- **Pegasus**: Winged horse ridden by the hero Bellerophon.
- **Phoenix**: Golden-red bird that regenerates.
- **Python**: Monstrous serpent guarding Delphi.
- **Satyrs**: Nature spirits with human male bodies, horse tails and ass ears.
- **Sirens**: Winged sea monsters with human female heads/torsos, luring sailors with song.
- **Typhon**: Giant with many animal heads, serpent hands/legs, wings and fire breath.

Typhon

"The defeat of the Gigantes by the gods angered Gaea (Earth), so she had intercourse with Tartarus and bore Typhon. He was a mixture of man and beast, the largest and strongest of all Gaea's children."

Bibliotheca, Pseudo-Apollodorus, 200 BCE

Typhon, the fearsome "father of all monsters", was a colossal serpentine being born from the Primordial forces Gaia (Earth) and Tartarus (Punishment), boasting 100 dragon heads and a deafening roar. In a legendary battle for cosmic authority, Typhon attempted to overthrow Zeus. An almighty battle commenced! The king of the gods ultimately defeated Typhon with a barrage of thunderbolts, imprisoning him beneath Mount Etna. With Etna experiencing a notable eruption in 396 BCE, it was clearly on Pseudo-Apollodorus's mind when he wrote *Bibliotheca* and reflected on volcanic power as a manifestation of primal, monstrous forces.

Echidna

"Whosoever met the Echidna, the day of doom would sweep him away."

Homeric Hymn to Apollo, Homer, 750 BCE

Known as the "mother of monsters", the she-dragon Echidna birthed a host of formidable creatures. With the head and torso of a woman and the tail of a coiling serpent, Echidna represented the illness, disease, rot and decay of Earth. Her monstrous offspring included the multi-headed dog Cerberus, the fire-breathing Chimera, the riddling Sphinx, the six-headed sea monster Scylla, the venomous Hydra and the giant serpent Python.

Medusa

The curse of Medusa remains a powerful myth from ancient Greece. Once a beautiful priestess with stunning golden hair, who served Athena, Medusa suffered a terrible transformation. After violating her vows of celibacy with Poseidon (in Athena's temple, the cheek), the enraged Athena cursed her for eternity. Medusa's beautiful blonde hair transformed to spitting venomous snakes and her gaze turned anyone who looked at her to stone! (The origin of the term "turn to stone".) Later in the legend, the hero Perseus used a mirrored shield to avoid her direct gaze, and cut Medusa's head clean off. From her severed neck sprang the winged horse Pegasus.

"Medusa was violated in Athena's shrine by Poseidon. Athena turned away and covered with her shield her virgin's eyes. And then for fitting punishment transformed the Gorgon's lovely hair to loathsome snakes."

Metamorphoses, Ovid, 8 BCE

Pegasus

"Bellerophon mounted Pegasus, his winged horse born of Medusa and Posidon, and flying into the air brought down the Chimera with his bow and arrows."

Bibliotheca, Pseudo-Apollodorus, 200 BCE

Renowned Greek hero Bellerophon was inseparable from his winged white stallion Pegasus. Together, they were asked by King Iobates to complete a perilous feat to kill the deadly Chimera, a fire-breathing monster with a lion's head, goat's body and a serpent's tail, which had been destroying the local villages of Lycia. Mounted on Pegasus, Bellerophon defeated the Chimera in a bloody battle, eventually suffocating it with a lead-tipped spear that melted by the monster's own flames. The killing secured Bellerophon's heroic legacy. Sadly, his attempt to fly to Mount Olympus on Pegasus led to his death.

The Minotaur

The tale of Theseus and the Minotaur is a Greek myth that popularized labyrinths as a cool way to tell a hero's story: think *Indiana Jones*, *Harry Potter* and *Inception*. A hero of Athens, young Theseus one day ventured to Crete. There, he fell in love with Cretan King Minos's daughter, Ariadne – and also learned of the king's cruel annual sacrifice of feeding young Athenian men and women to the Minotaur, a monstrous creature with the head of a bull and the body of a man, housed in a vast labyrinth. Determined to end this brutal tradition, Theseus volunteered to enter the maze. Ariadne provided him with a ball of string so he could find his way back out of the labyrinth – if he slayed the Minotaur. Theseus entered the maze, found the Minotaur, and after a bloody struggle, killed the beast. Theseus then successfully navigated his way out using the thread. He left Crete with Ariadne and the freed Athenian youths (abandoning Ariadne along the way!). This tale teaches us that freedom awaits those who confront their inner monsters. And the importance of string.

Argos

"Argos, the hound of Odysseus, of the steadfast heart."

The Odyssey, Homer, 750 BCE

Argos, Odysseus's loyal hunting dog, appears in Homer's *The Odyssey*. After his master's 20-year absence, Argos is neglected and old, lying on a dung heap, and rife with vermin; however, he is the only one to immediately recognize Odysseus upon his heroic return to Ithaca, despite his master's disguise as a beggar. With a feeble wag of his tail and a drop of his ears, Argos acknowledges his long-lost master is finally home. Odysseus, unable to reveal himself, sheds a secret tear for the unwavering loyalty of his old, dying dog. Argos dies shortly after seeing his beloved master, his faithfulness rewarded by a final moment of recognition.

The Cyclops

Returning home to Ithaca, victorious from battle after a 10-year war with the Trojans, Odysseus and his crew first found themselves shipwrecked on an island home to Cyclopes – monstrous one-eyed giants. When trapped in the cave of Polyphemus, a particularly monstrous Cyclopes who began eating his men, Odysseus offered the giant potent wine until drunk. When Polyphemus asked his name, Odysseus said "Ou tis" (no one). As Polyphemus slept, Odysseus blinded the creature's giant eye with a stake. Polyphemus's cries of "No one is attacking me!" confused the other Cyclopes who came to help, allowing Odysseus and his crew to escape.

The Sphinx

"What goes on four feet in the morning, two feet at noon, and three feet in the evening?"

This is the classic riddle set by the Sphinx, a creature with a lion's body and a woman's head, as she sat perched outside the gates of the city of Thebes, the ancient Greek city, just north of Athens. In order to permit passage through the city, the Sphinx would require the solution to the conundrum. Anyone who failed to answer correctly, the Sphinx devoured. No one ever got it right, and the city was dying, until Oedipus, a supposed orphan, arrived one day and solved the puzzle. The Sphinx, in her defeat, threw herself from a cliff. As a reward for freeing the city, Oedipus is made king and married the widowed queen, Jocasta... spoiler alert!... his own mother.

And the answer to the riddle is... Man. (Four feet refers to a baby crawling on their hands and knees. Two feet represents an adult walking upright on two legs. Three feet symbolizes an elderly person using a cane for support.)

Monsters & Mythological Creatures

The Nemean Lion

"The Nemean Lion whom Hera, the queenly wife of Zeus, trained up to be a plague to mankind. Nevertheless, the force of strong Heracles subdued him."

Theogony, Hesiod, 800 BCE

Heracles' first and famed labour (out of 12) tasked him with slaying the Nemean Lion, a fearsome creature with impenetrable golden fur and razor claws. It loved nothing more than terrorizing the villagers of Nemea. This was a job for Heracles!

Tracking the monster to its two-entranced den, Heracles blocked one of the entrances. Surprising the lion, he tried beating it with his club, but soon realized no weapon could pierce its hide. So he strangled it with his bare hands, losing a finger in the fight. Heracles then skinned the beast using its own claws and wore its pelt for protection. King Eurystheus, who had set the task, was terrified by Heracles' bloody return to the village in the great lion's skin. The gods later immortalized the lion as the constellation Leo.

CHAPTER FOUR

A Lasting Legacy

Democracy

"In a democracy, there is, first, that most splendid of virtues, equality before the law."

Histories, Herodotus, 460 BCE

Around 508 BCE, ancient Athens, a society steeped in the narratives of Greek mythology, sparked a political earthquake by giving birth to the first known democracy, a word that comes from two Greek words that mean people (*demos*) and rule (*kratos*). Dissatisfied with elite dominance, Athenians boldly introduced a system where male citizens actively shaped their city's future through open assemblies and voting. While the legends of gods and heroes didn't directly cause this historic shift, the myths permeating their culture explored themes of justice, civic duty and the perils of tyranny, suggesting a connection between Greece's foundational mythology and its pioneering democracy. These stories, alongside a vibrant tradition of philosophical debate and reason, fostered a culture where the concept of shared rule and accountability could take root and flourish.

Olympic Games

"Greatness of mind and fortune too,
Th' Olympick trophies shew:
Both their several parts must do
In the noble chace of fame."

Olympian 1, Pindar, 476 BC

The original Olympic Games, a significant religious festival honouring Zeus, began in Olympia, Greece, in 776 BCE. Held every four years, the Games drew athletes from all Greek city-states. Initially, a single-day event with just one foot race, the Games soon expanded to include running, wrestling, boxing, the pentathlon and chariot racing. Coroebus of Elis was the first Olympic champion in 776 BCE, winning the 192-meter race – covering one length of the stadium in Olympia. He received an olive wreath for his efforts. Medals were given in the first modern Olympic Games in 1896.

Metamorphosis

"My mind is bent to tell of bodies changed into new forms."

Metamorphoses, Ovid, 8 BCE

Metamorphosis, the act of transforming something, often into a completely different form, is a fundamental element of Greek myths, typically occurring through divine intervention or sorcery, and rarely being voluntary. Indeed, countless transformations abound – changes of sex or into inanimate objects, stars and constellations, flora and fauna, animals and insects, as seen in the examples of Io becoming a cow; Callisto a bear; Actaeon a deer; the daughters of Minyas bats; Tereus, Procne and Philomela birds; and Daphne a tree.

Sisyphus

"Know that no one is free, except Zeus."

Prometheus Bound, Aeschylus, 479 BCE

A Sisyphean task is a chore that is laborious, futile and never-ending, a job characterized by endless repetition and a lack of progress. Modern life is one long Sisyphean ordeal, isn't it?

The term's origins lie in the myth of Sisyphus, the cunning and deceitful king of Corinth, an ancient Greek city, who angered Zeus by cheating death (twice). Zeus condemned Sisyphus to an eternity of a seemingly pointless and exhausting task in the Underworld: he was forced to roll an enormous boulder up a steep hill. Whenever the boulder reached the summit it would roll back down to the bottom. Sisyphus then had to start all over again, repeating this agonizing and ultimately fruitless cycle for all eternity.

The A to Z of Mythology: Part II

- **Hermetic**: Secret, magical (from Hermes, the god of messengers, trade and sports).
- **Hypnosis**: Sleep-like state (from Hypnos, the personification of sleep, and the brother of Thanatos (Death)).
- **Lunatic**: Insane (from Selene, the Titan goddess of the moon, and her Roman equivalent Luna; historically associated with the moon's influence on the mind).
- **Mentor**: Wise advisor (from Mentor, loyal friend of Odysseus who was entrusted with the care of Odysseus's son Telemachus).
- **Museum**: Art/science institution (from the Muses, the nine goddesses of the arts, sciences and inspiration).
- **Narcissist**: Self-obsessed (from Narcissus, a beautiful youth who fell in love with his own reflection, later turning into the narcissus flower).

- **Nemesis**: Revenge, downfall (from Nemesis, the Greek goddess of divine retribution against those who succumb to hubris (arrogance before the gods)).
- **Panic**: Sudden terror (from Pan, the god of the wild, shepherds, flocks, nature, rustic music and impromptus; often associated with causing sudden, irrational fear).
- **Pandora's box**: Source of troubles (from Pandora, the first mortal woman created by Hephaestus on Zeus's orders; she released all the evils into the world when she opened a jar).
- **Phobia**: Intense fear (from Phobos, the personification of fear and terror, and the brother of Deimos (Dread)).
- **Tantalize**: Tease with unattainability (from Tantalus, who was punished by being made to stand in a pool of water beneath a fruit tree that was out of reach).
- **Titanic**: Huge, powerful (from the Titans, the predecessors of the Olympian gods).

Temples of the Gods

Many of the ancient Greek temples and landmarks still stand, and can be enjoyed today.

- **Parthenon, Athens (447 BCE)**
  Dedicated to Athena, the Parthenon, on top of the Acropolis, is Greece's most popular tourist attraction today.
- **Temple of Olympian Zeus, Athens (527 BCE)**
  Once a colossal temple, only ruins remain.
- **Sanctuary of Delphi, Mount Parnassus (700 BCE)**
  Home to the famed Oracle of Apollo, the sanctuary was once a crucial religious centre.
- **Archaia Olympia, Elis (590 BCE)**
  The birthplace of the Olympic Games, dedicated to Zeus.
- **Temple of Hephaestus, Athens (415 BCE)**
  A Doric peripteral temple dedicated to Hephaestus, the god of fire and metal.

⁂ **Temple of Poseidon, Sounion (444 BCE)**
Perched on a cliff overlooking the Aegean Sea, this temple honoured Poseidon, god of the sea.

⁂ **Temple of Hera, Olympia (590 BCE)**
Dedicated to Hera, queen of the gods and goddess of marriage.

⁂ **Temple of Artemis, Ephesus (550 BCE)**
One of the Seven Wonders of the Ancient World, dedicated to Artemis, goddess of the moon.

⁂ **Sanctuary of Demeter and Persephone, Eleusis (600 BCE)**
The site of the Eleusinian Mysteries, honouring the goddesses of agriculture and the Underworld.

Mythos

"The Greeks created gods that were in their image: warlike but creative, wise but ferocious, loving but jealous, tender but brutal, compassionate but vengeful."

Mythos: The Greek Myths Reimagined, Stephen Fry, 2017

Since 2017, Britain's most beloved, most intelligent and most funniest national treasure, Stephen Fry, has released four acclaimed and bestselling books from his Greek myths series: *Mythos*, *Heroes*, *Troy* and *Odyssey*. Each book is as entertaining and engrossing as the next, making the myths understandable and accessible in a way rarely done with classical texts and tales. "Greek myths understand that whoever created this baffling world, with its cruelties, wonders, caprices, beauties, madness, and injustice, must themselves have been cruel, wonderful, capricious, beautiful, mad, and unjust," Fry states in the book.

Percy Jackson

"English literature draws heavily on Greek mythology. It always has."

Rick Riordan, rickriordan.com

With over 30 million copies sold in more than 37 languages, the *Percy Jackson* series of fantasy novels is now the leading retelling of Greek myths for young modern audiences, where immortals and monsters cause all sorts of mischief in 21st-century New York. Across seven books, the story follows Perseus "Percy" Jackson, a 12-year-old boy who learns he is the son of the Greek god, Poseidon. "I used Percy Jackson in the ways that Greek myths have always been used – to explain things that are difficult to explain," Rick Riordan told the *Guardian* in 2016.

Comic Heroes

Comic-book heroes, so prevalent in the 21st century, and Greek mythological heroes, share DNA. Batman, with his tragic origin story, is Heracles. Tony Stark (Iron Man) is Daedalus – a mad scientist. (Similar to Tony Stark's Iron Man suit, Daedalus created Icarus's wings.) Superman is Achilles – a powerful demigod, with a fatal flaw; Kryptonite is his Achilles' heel. And Wonder Woman is the daughter of Queen Hippolyta, the Amazon queen. Spider-Man is reminiscent of Arachne, a mortal woman so skilled in weaving that she challenged Athena and was transformed into a spider as punishment. And Thor? He's Zeus, clearly.

"I'm not the first person to say this, but I've long said that comic books are the modern equivalent of our Greek myths."

David S. Goyer, Collider.com, 2014

The Other Homer

"There's a little Homer Simpson in all of us."

Homer Simpson in "Homer's Odyssey",
The Simpsons (1990)

The first episode of cartoon series *The Simpsons*, "Homer's Odyssey" draws its title from Homer's epic Greek poem, *The Odyssey*. Here, Homer Simpson embarks on a challenging quest to improve safety in Springfield after losing his job at the local nuclear power plant, mirroring Odysseus's arduous journey. (Sort of!) Creator Matt Groening named his iconic character (and his own son) after his father, Homer, who was named after the ancient Greek poet.

Global Branding

Many major global corporations have drawn on Greek myths for the names of their products:

- ⁂ **Ajax**: Hero of the Trojan War, known for his power, the name of a household grime cleaner.
- ⁂ **Venus**: Leading female razor brand, named after the goddess of love and beauty.
- ⁂ **Pandora**: The first woman in myth, lends her name to a famous jewellery brand.
- ⁂ **Nike**: Greek goddess of victory, is the namesake of the global No.1 sports brand.
- ⁂ **The Amazons**: Legendary race of warrior women, give their name to the world's top e-commerce company.
- ⁂ **Hermes**: Renowned fashion brand, takes its name from the god of travellers.

"I chose the name 'Apollo' after perusing a book of mythology at home one evening in 1960. The image of Apollo riding his chariot across the Sun was appropriate to the grand scale of the mission."

Origins of NASA Names, Abe Silverstein, 1976

NASA's Apollo

When NASA launched its historic mission to send three astronauts to the Moon in July 1969, they fittingly named it Apollo, after the Greek god of light, knowledge and archery, whose legendary aim symbolized the mission's precision. Continuing this celestial tradition, NASA announced in May 2023 its plan to return to the Moon by 2030 under the Artemis program. Artemis, the Greek goddess of the Moon and Apollo's twin sister, embodies the spirit of the 250,000-mile journey. This ambitious endeavour aims to land the first woman and person of colour on the Moon, establish a sustainable lunar base, and pave the way for future human exploration of Mars. God speed!

"Subtle as Sphinx; as sweet and musical
As bright Apollo's lute, strung with his hair;
And when Love speaks, the voice of all the gods
Makes heaven drowsy with the harmony.
Never durst poet touch a pen to write
Until his ink were tempered with Love's sighs."

Love's Labour's Lost, William Shakespeare, 1590s

Greco-Roman Gods

Though he was a Roman poet, Ovid's *Metamorphoses* is still considered one of the most important mythological texts in history, and was the first to blend stories of Greek and Roman gods, heroes, battles and quests. A 15-book Latin narrative poem, *Metamorphoses* chronicles the history of the world using 250 myths, a tome that influenced Geoffrey Chaucer and William Shakespeare, to name but two. To honour Ovid's marriage of Greco-Roman tales, here is the list of *interpretatio graeca*, the Roman counterparts of Greek gods, established as the Roman Empire devoured Greece around 200 BCE.

⁂ **Zeus**: King of the gods ~ *Jupiter*

⁂ **Hera**: Queen of the gods ~ *Juno*

⁂ **Poseidon**: God of the sea ~ *Neptune*

⁂ **Hades**: God of the Underworld ~ *Pluto*

⁂ **Demeter**: Goddess of agriculture ~ *Ceres*

⁂ **Athena**: Goddess of wisdom and strategic warfare ~ *Minerva*

- ⁂ **Apollo**: God of music, poetry, light, healing and prophecy ~ *Apollo*
- ⁂ **Artemis**: Goddess of the moon ~ *Diana*
- ⁂ **Ares**: God of war ~ *Mars*
- ⁂ **Aphrodite**: Goddess of love and beauty ~ *Venus*
- ⁂ **Hermes**: Messenger of the gods ~ *Mercury*
- ⁂ **Hephaestus**: God of fire ~ *Vulcan*
- ⁂ **Dionysus**: God of wine ~ *Bacchus*
- ⁂ **Eros**: God of desire and erotic love ~ *Cupid*
- ⁂ **Nike**: Goddess of victory ~ *Victoria*
- ⁂ **Persephone**: Queen of the Underworld and goddess of springtime ~ *Proserpina*
- ⁂ **Pan**: God of nature ~ *Faunus*
- ⁂ **Hecate**: Goddess of magic ~ *Trivia*

Lady Liberty

Cast onto a bronze plaque and mounted inside New York's Statue of Liberty, is a poem entitled "The New Colossus", written by American poet Emma Lazarus in 1883. The sonnet refers to the "Colossus of Rhodes", a 33-meter iron-bronze statue of the sun god Helios, erected in 280 BCE to celebrate Rhodes' victory in battle. It was one of the Seven Wonders of the Ancient World. It stood for just 54 years before an earthquake toppled it in 226 BCE. Even in ruins, its immense size inspired awe for centuries – including the creators of Lady Liberty.

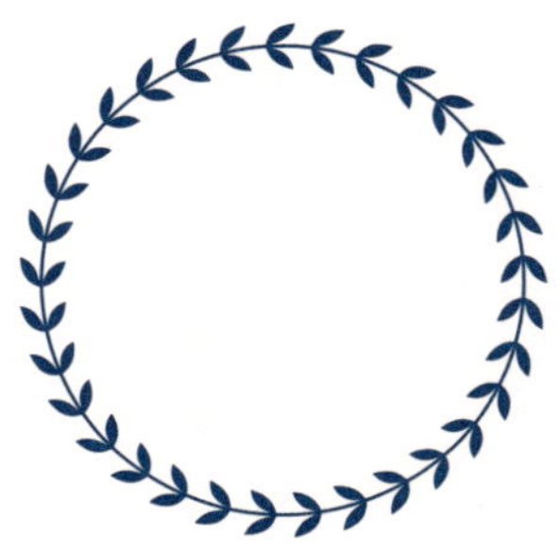

"Not like the brazen giant of Greek fame,
With conquering limbs astride from land to land;
Here at our sea-washed, sunset gates shall stand
A mighty woman with a torch, whose flame
Is the imprisoned lightning, and her name...
With silent lips. 'Give me your tired, your poor,
Your huddled masses yearning to breathe free,
The wretched refuse of your teeming shore.
Send these, the homeless, tempest-tost to me,
I lift my lamp beside the golden door!'"

"The New Colossus", Emma Lazarus, 1883

Pygmalion

Pygmalion – the concept of falling in love with one's own creation – originates from the Greek myth of Pygmalion, a gifted sculptor from Cyprus, and his ivory statue, Galatea. Pygmalion created the statue, inspired by Aphrodite, an unparalleled beauty, after he grew disillusioned with the imperfections of mortal women. He soon fell deeply in love with it. He adorned it with gifts, dressed it in exquisite garments, and spoke to it as though she were real, and wished she would come to life. Witnessing his devotion, Aphrodite answered his prayers. Upon kissing the statue, Pygmalion witnessed Galatea's ivory transform into warm flesh, and his creation became alive as a beautiful woman.

From mythological origins, such as Aphrodite's birth from her father's "sea foam" and Eve's creation from Adam's rib, the Pygmalion archetype appears in literature (Shakespeare's *The Winter's Tale*), theatre (*My Fair Lady*), animation (*Pinocchio*) and modern cinema (*Pretty Woman*, *Mannequin*, *The Devil Wears Prada*, *Weird Science*). One of the most prominent reinterpretations of the myth is in the eponymous play by George Bernard Shaw in 1912.

"Any moment might be our last. Everything is more beautiful because we're doomed. You will never be lovelier than you are now. We will never be here again."

Achilles in *The Iliad*, Homer, 750 BCE